This page intentionally left blank

TABLE OF CONTENTS

EXECUTIVE SUMMARY

On January 16, 2015, President Barack Obama issued Executive Order 13688, "Federal Support for Local Law Enforcement Equipment Acquisition" (EO), to identify actions that can improve Federal support for the appropriate use, acquisition, and transfer of controlled equipment by State, local, and Tribal law enforcement agencies (LEAs). The EO established a Federal interagency Law Enforcement Equipment Working Group, which consulted with stakeholders and deliberated to develop the recommendations described in this report.

- ***Establishment of Federal Government-wide Prohibited Equipment Lists.*** The Prohibited Equipment List identifies categories of equipment that LEAs will not be able to acquire via transfer from Federal agencies or purchase using Federally-provided funds (e.g., Tracked Armored Vehicles, Bayonets, Grenade Launchers, Large Caliber Weapons and Ammunition). The Prohibited Equipment List will take effect upon transmission of the recommendations to the President.

- ***Establishment of Federal Government-wide Controlled Equipment Lists.*** The Controlled Equipment List identifies categories of equipment (e.g., Wheeled Armored or Tactical Vehicles, Specialized Firearms and Ammunition, Explosives and Pyrotechnics, Riot Equipment) that LEAs, other than those solely serving schools with grades ranging from kindergarten through grade 12, may acquire if they provide additional information, certifications, and assurances. While inclusion on these lists would not preclude an LEA from using other funds for such acquisitions, the Working Group's report urges LEAs to give careful consideration to the appropriateness of acquiring such equipment for their communities.

- ***Harmonization of Federal Acquisition Processes.*** All Federal equipment acquisition programs must require LEAs that apply for controlled equipment to provide mandatory information in their application, including a detailed justification with a clear and persuasive explanation of the need for the controlled equipment, the availability of the requested controlled equipment to LEA in its inventory or through other means, certifications that appropriate protocols and training requirements have been adopted, evidence of the civilian governing body's review and approval or concurrence of the LEA's acquisition of the requested controlled equipment, and whether the LEA has been or is in violation of civil rights and other statutes, regulations, or programmatic terms. Ongoing coordination among the various Federal agencies will ensure that a uniform process is in place to assess the adequacy of the justification in each application.

- ***Required Protocols and Training for LEAs that Acquire Controlled Equipment.*** LEAs that acquire controlled equipment through Federal resources must adopt General Policing Standards, including community policing, constitutional policing, and community input and impact principles. LEAs also must adopt Specific Controlled Equipment Standards on the appropriate use, supervision, evaluation, accountability, transparency, and operation of controlled equipment. LEAs must train its personnel on General Policing and Specific Controlled Equipment Standards on an annual basis.

- *Required Information Collection and Retention for Controlled Equipment Use in Significant Incidents.* LEAs must collect and retain certain information when the LEA uses controlled equipment in operations or actions that are deemed to be Significant Incidents. LEAs also must collect and retain information when allegations of unlawful or inappropriate police actions involving the use of controlled equipment trigger a Federal compliance review of the LEA. Upon request, the LEA must provide a copy of this information to the Federal agency that supplied the equipment/funds. This information also should be made available to the community the LEA serves in accordance with the LEAs applicable policies and protocols.

- *Approval for Third-Party Transfers or Sales.* LEAs must receive approval from the Federal agency that supplied the funds or equipment before selling or transferring controlled equipment. Third-party LEAs acquiring controlled equipment must provide to the Federal Government the same information, certifications, and assurances that were required of selling/transferring LEAs. Sales or transfers to non-LEAs are restricted to certain types of controlled equipment that do not pose a great risk of danger or harm to the community if acquired by non-LEAs.

- *Increase Federal Government Oversight and Compliance.* The Federal Government will expand its monitoring and compliance capabilities to ensure that LEAs acquiring controlled equipment adhere to protocols, training, information collection and retention, and other requirements proposed by the recommendations this report. Additionally, the Federal Government will create a permanent interagency working group to, among other things, evaluate the Controlled and Prohibited Equipment Lists for additions and deletions, track controlled equipment purchased with Federal resources, develop Government-wide criteria for evaluating applications and conducting compliance reviews, and sharing information on sanctions and violations by LEA applicants. The United States Digital Service will assist Federal agencies in the creation of a database that tracks information about controlled equipment acquired through Federal programs.

These recommendations, if accepted and approved by the President, will be implemented by the beginning of Fiscal Year 2016 (October 1, 2015); the Prohibited Equipment List will take effect upon transmission of the recommendations to the President. The recommendations on protocols, training, acquisitions, and transfers and sales to third parties apply to all items on the Controlled Equipment List and are triggered when an LEA acquires controlled equipment using Federal resources beginning in Fiscal Year 2016. Within 45 days after the President receives these recommendations, Federal agencies will meet with stakeholders to further discuss the specifics of the recommendations and receive feedback on the potential approaches to implementing them. By the end of Fiscal Year 2015, Federal agencies will provide an update to the President on the progress of implementing the recommendations and any additional recommendations, suggestions, or clarifications to be considered based on stakeholder feedback.

BACKGROUND

For decades, the Federal Government has provided, and continues to provide, State, local, and tribal law enforcement agencies (LEAs) with funding and equipment, either directly or indirectly, to support and augment LEA operations. This equipment ranges from standard office supplies and administrative items (e.g., desks or computers) to weapons and military or "military-style" equipment (e.g., firearms, ammunition, and tactical vehicles). The purpose of providing this equipment to LEAs via Federal programs is to enhance and improve the LEAs' mission to protect and serve their communities. Equipment provided through Federal sources has become a critical component of LEAs' inventory, especially as fiscal challenges have mounted and other sources of equipment and funding have diminished. LEAs rely on Federally-acquired equipment to conduct a variety of law enforcement operations including hostage rescue, special operations, response to threats of terrorism, and fugitive apprehension. Use of Federally-acquired equipment also enhances the safety of officers who are often called upon to respond to dangerous or violent situations; being improperly equipped in such operations can have life-threatening consequences, both for the law enforcement personnel and the public they are charged with protecting.

Over the last several years, however, community members, LEA leaders, civil rights advocates, and elected leaders have voiced concerns about what has been described as the "militarization" of law enforcement due to the types of equipment at times deployed by LEAs and the nature of those deployments.[1] The most widely publicized example of this phenomenon occurred during the widespread protests in Ferguson, Missouri, in August 2014. At times, the law enforcement response to those protests was characterized as a "military-style" operation, as evidenced by videos and photographs that showed law enforcement officers atop armored vehicles, wearing uniforms often associated with the military, and holding military-type weapons.[2] Even before the events in Ferguson, however, civil rights organizations conducted significant research on the perceived harms of "militarization" of civilian law enforcement agencies in the United States and advocated for systemic change.[3]

In August 2014, the President ordered a government-wide review of military equipment, including personnel carriers and high-caliber firearms, provided to LEAs.[4] As a result of this directive, the Executive Office of the President, in December 2014, released, "Review: Federal

---

[1] See, e.g., https://www.aclu.org/feature/war-comes-home.

[2] http://www.washingtonpost.com/politics/militarized-police-in-ferguson-unsettles-some-pentagon-gives-cities-equipment/2014/08/14/4651f670-2401-11e4-86ca-6f03cbd15c1a_story.html.

[3] .https://www.aclu.org/feature/war-comes-home.

[4] In addition to the Federal Review, Congress conducted hearings on how Federal programs provide equipment to LEAs. On September 9, 2014, the U.S. Senate Committee on Homeland Security and Governmental Affairs held a hearing on "Oversight of Federal Programs for Equipping State and Local Law Enforcement." On November 13, 2014, the U.S. House of Representatives Armed Services Committee held a hearing on "The Department of Defense Excess Property Program in Support of U.S. Law Enforcement Agencies: An Overview of DOD Authorities, Roles, Responsibilities, and Implementation of Section 1033 of the 1997 National Defense Authorization Act."

Support for Local Law Enforcement Equipment Acquisition" (Federal Review).[5] The Federal Review identified and assessed multiple Federal programs that provide equipment to LEAs through excess and surplus equipment transfers, asset forfeiture programs, or Federal grant programs. LEAs may acquire equipment from the Federal Government from excess accumulations from the U.S. Department of Defense (DOD) or surplus accumulations from the U.S. General Services Administration's (GSA) Federal Surplus Personal Property Donation Program, purchase it using grant funding provided by the U.S. Department of Justice (DOJ) or the U.S. Department of Homeland Security (DHS), or purchase it using asset forfeiture-related funding from DOJ or the U.S. Department of the Treasury (Treasury), among other Federal programs.[6]

The findings of the Federal Review highlighted a "lack of consistency in how Federal programs are structured, implemented, audited, and informed by conversations with stakeholders."[7] The Federal Review also identified several areas of focus that could better ensure the appropriate use of Federal programs to maximize the safety and security of law enforcement officers and the communities they serve, including: (1) harmonizing Federal programs so that they have consistent and transparent policies; (2) mandating that LEAs that participate in Federal equipment programs receive necessary training; (3) ensuring that those LEAs have policies in place that address appropriate use and employment of controlled equipment; and (4) requiring that those LEAs also adopt policies addressing protection of civil rights and civil liberties in the use of equipment.[8] Finally, the Federal Review recommended the issuance of an Executive Order identifying actions to enhance Federal support to LEAs regarding the acquisition of controlled equipment.

1. EXECUTIVE ORDER 13688

On January 16, 2015, the President issued Executive Order No. 13688, "Federal Support for Local Law Enforcement Equipment Acquisition" (Executive Order or EO).[9] The EO emphasizes the need to better coordinate Federal support for the acquisition of certain Federal equipment by State, local, and Tribal law enforcement agencies and ensure that LEAs have proper training regarding the appropriate use of that equipment, including training on the protection of civil rights and civil liberties. Specifically, the EO identifies 11 issue areas for inquiry, which can be divided into five general categories:

---

[5] "Review: Federal Support for Local Law Enforcement Equipment Acquisition," December 2014 (Federal Review).
[6] See Appendix B for an overview of applicable Federal programs.
[7] Federal Review, p. 3.
[8] Federal Review, p. 6.
[9] See Appendix A.

Equipment Lists

- Develop a consistent, Government-wide list of controlled equipment allowable for acquisition by LEAs, as well as a list of those items that can only be transferred with special authorization and use limitations.

Policies, Training, and Protocols for Controlled Equipment

- Develop policies to ensure that LEAs abide by any limitations or affirmative obligations imposed on the acquisition of controlled equipment or receipt of funds to purchase controlled equipment from the Federal Government and the obligations resulting from receipt of Federal financial assistance.

- Require that LEAs participating in Federal controlled equipment programs receive necessary training regarding appropriate use of controlled equipment and the implementation of obligations resulting from receipt of Federal financial assistance, including training on the protection of civil rights and civil liberties.

- Require after-action analysis reports for significant incidents involving Federally-provided or Federally-funded controlled equipment.

Acquisition Process for Controlled Equipment

- Harmonize Federal programs so that they have consistent and transparent policies with respect to the acquisition of controlled equipment by LEAs.

- Require local civilian government (non-police) review of and authorization for LEAs' request for or acquisition of controlled equipment.

Transfer, Sale, Return, and Disposal of Controlled Equipment

- Ensure a process for returning specified controlled equipment that was acquired from the Federal Government when no longer needed by an LEA.

- Create a process to monitor the sale or transfer of controlled equipment from the Federal Government or controlled equipment purchased with funds from the Federal Government by LEAs to third parties.

Oversight, Compliance, and Implementation

- Establish a process to review and approve proposed additions or deletions to the list of controlled equipment.

- Plan the creation of a database that includes information about controlled equipment purchased or acquired through Federal programs.

- Provide uniform standards for suspending LEAs from Federal controlled equipment programs for specified violations of law, including civil rights laws, and ensure that those standards are implemented consistently across agencies.

To examine these issues, the Executive Order established a Federal interagency Law Enforcement Equipment Working Group (Working Group), which was charged with "providing specific recommendations to the President regarding actions that can be taken to improve the provision of Federal support for the acquisition of managed equipment by LEAs."[10] The Working Group is co-chaired by the Attorney General, the Secretary of Defense, and the Secretary of Homeland Security. The Working Group's membership is composed of the Secretaries of the Treasury, Interior, and Education; the Administrator of General Services; the Directors of the Domestic Policy Council, the Office of National Drug Control Policy, and the Office of Management and Budget; the Assistants to the President for Intergovernmental Affairs and Public Engagement, and for Homeland Security and Counterterrorism; and the Assistant to the President and Chief of Staff of the Office of the Vice President. The Executive Director of the Working Group is the Assistant Attorney General for the Office of Justice Programs, who was appointed by the Attorney General, as directed by Section 2(c) of the Executive Order.

2. STAKEHOLDERS

Critical to the Working Group's development of recommendations and implementation plans in support of the Executive Order was outreach to and engagement of stakeholders.[11] As tasked by the Executive Order, the Working Group throughout the recommendation development process solicited input from numerous stakeholder groups, associations, and concerned individuals representing law enforcement, civil rights and civil liberties organizations, State, local, and Tribal government, and academia.[12] This outreach effort built on and expanded the stakeholder engagement that was conducted as part of the Federal Review. Stakeholders were also encouraged to submit written comments to the Working Group.

The majority of the stakeholders who provided comments to the Working Group expressed support for the appropriate use of controlled equipment by LEAs and the development of LEA policies for the procurement, deployment, and general use of the equipment. A majority of stakeholders who provided comments also indicated their support of mandatory training for LEAs on the appropriate use and deployment of such equipment. Stakeholders also articulated that training on civil rights and civil liberties is necessary to prevent potential civil or human rights violations resulting from the misuse of controlled equipment. These comments and suggestions were carefully considered and incorporated into this report, as appropriate.

In addition to stakeholder outreach, in April 2015, the Executive Director of the Working Group convened a focus group composed of representatives of relevant stakeholder groups. Further, the Working Group engaged the Institute for Intergovernmental Research (IIR), a non-profit organization specializing in criminal justice issues, and its subject matter experts to assist in the drafting of this report.

---

[10] See Appendix A.
[11] See Appendix A.
[12] See Appendix C for a representative list of stakeholders that the Working Group engaged.

RECOMMENDATIONS

The recommendations presented in this report are the product of a 120-day process during which the Working Group conducted an in-depth examination of existing Federal procedures, policies, and oversight mechanisms related to the provision of controlled equipment to LEAs. The Working Group also studied the use of Federally-acquired equipment by LEAs and the impact it has on members of the community. Through this process, the Working Group developed a comprehensive set of programmatic and policy recommendations that lay out a blueprint for positive change. Following these recommendations will improve Federal equipment acquisition programs and allow Federal agencies to better support their state and local law enforcement partners and the communities they serve. [13]

In developing these recommendations, the Working Group was cognizant of the seemingly competing priorities of a diverse set of stakeholders. Equipment provided through Federal acquisition programs is extremely important to LEAs, especially in times of fiscal uncertainty when other resources are unavailable. LEAs frequently depend on this equipment for law enforcement operations to prevent crime, ensure officer safety, and protect and serve the public. Yet, in some neighborhoods and communities, incidents of misuse, overuse, and inappropriate use of controlled equipment occur, and the resulting strain placed on the community and its relationship with law enforcement is severe. Although law enforcement as a whole should not be castigated for the actions of some, the Federal Government has a responsibility when significant issues arise to examine its equipment programs to determine what changes are needed to ensure appropriate use.

The Working Group also was aware that creating new requirements or changing existing procedures could have a tangible effect on the workload of LEAs, State and Tribal Coordinators, and Federal agency staff. This burden likely would fall hardest on smaller LEAs that do not have the capacity to quickly adapt to Federal mandates, as well as on large LEAs that cover populous areas and conduct a significant number of operations. To the extent possible, the Working Group therefore attempted to work within existing processes so as to avoid creating additional administrative burdens for law enforcement.

With these considerations in mind, the Working Group submits the following recommendations for the President's consideration.[14]

---

[13] These recommendations are intended to apply also to Tribal LEAs that acquire controlled equipment through Federal resources. Before the recommendations are implemented with respect to Tribal LEAs, the Working Group will ensure that the specific requirements triggered by potential changes to Federal programs affecting sovereign tribes, including appropriate Tribal consultation, are met.

These recommendations do not apply to controlled equipment acquired or used solely for the purpose of participating in Federal Task Forces in which LEA personnel are cross-designated as Federal law enforcement agents or operate under the policies or direction of a Federal law enforcement agency.

[14] The recommendations in this report are proposals for the President's consideration, even though they are written as mandatory (or, in some cases, permissive) requirements.

1. EQUIPMENT LISTS

Develop a consistent, Government-wide list of controlled equipment allowable for acquisition by LEAs, as well as a list of those items that can only be transferred with special authorization and use limitations.

Executive Order 13688, Section (3)(i)

The Executive Order initially tasked the Working Group with developing a Government-wide list identifying the types of equipment that LEAs could acquire through Federal programs, as well as establishing a process to review and approve proposed additions and deletions to these lists. With slight modification, the recommendations described below were provided in an interim report to the President on March 16, 2015, in accordance with Section 4 of the EO.

To develop a recommended listing of controlled equipment available to LEAs, as well as a list of prohibited equipment, the Working Group first examined the existing Federal agency equipment lists to determine the types or categories of equipment that are eligible for transfer or purchase by LEAs through federal acquisition programs. The lists that the Working Group reviewed included DHS's Authorized Equipment List (AEL),[15] DOJ's Justice Assistance Grant (JAG) program,[16] and the DOD 1033 program[17] (based on the Department of State Munitions Control List and the Department of Commerce Control List). The Working Group also reviewed program guidance from the Treasury and the DOJ Asset Forfeiture offices, GSA, the U.S. Department of the Interior (DOI), and ONDCP. These lists were also compared against the U.S. Munitions List (22 U.S.C. § 2278; 22 C.F.R. Part 121)[18] and the Commerce Control List (15 C.F.R. Part 774)[19] to identify any other items that should be considered within this review process.

The equipment lists reviewed by the Working Group were expansive and included routine items such as office equipment, cameras, and plywood; equipment that may be more hazardous but does not have a particular law enforcement purpose, such as locomotives; and equipment that may have militaristic connotations, such as armored personnel carriers, high-powered assault rifles, and aircraft. The Working Group focused on items that may have an operational law enforcement nexus/justification, further narrowing the results to identify equipment that merited discussion for inclusion in either a controlled or prohibited list. Items that were already prohibited and clearly had no law enforcement nexus or justification, such as nuclear weapons, are not included on the Working Group's recommended prohibited list. Equipment not listed on the recommended Prohibited or Controlled Equipment Lists are still subject to the restrictions and prohibitions set by the applicable Federal agency's guidelines, regulations, and statutory

---

[15] http://www.fema.gov/media-library-data/20130726-1825-25045-7138/fema_preparedness_grants_authorized_equipment_list.pdf
[16] https://www.bja.gov/Funding/JAGIdentifiers.pdf
[17] http://www.dispositionservices.dla.mil/leso/Documents/propertyavailable.pdf
[18] http://www.gpo.gov/fdsys/granule/CFR-2012-title22-vol1/CFR-2012-title22-vol1-part121.
[19] http://www.gpo.gov/fdsys/pkg/CFR-2012-title15-vol2/pdf/CFR-2012-title15-vol2-part774-appNo-.pdf.

authority. For example, nuclear weapons will remain on DOD's restricted (i.e., prohibited) list even though they were not specifically included in the Working Group's prohibited list.

Based on the types of equipment identified in these lists and the comments received from stakeholders, the Working Group developed a suggested Government-wide prohibited equipment list and a controlled equipment list to enhance consistency across Federal agencies and programs. The Working Group balanced the law enforcement need and utility for the equipment with the potential negative impact on the community if the equipment was used arbitrarily or inappropriately. Throughout this process, however, Working Group members emphasized that these lists should be considered a baseline, or "floor" level, for each Federal agency; that is, Federal agencies and programs may enact stricter guidelines, consistent with the underlying legal framework and purposes of the programs at issue. For example, the Homeland Security Grant Program (HSGP) prohibits the purchase of firearms with program funding; although certain firearms are identified on the controlled equipment list, they will remain unavailable for purchase through the HSGP.[20]

The inclusion of items on the recommended Prohibited or Controlled Equipment Lists does not preclude an LEA from using State, local, Tribal, or other funds for such purchases. However, when non-Federal funds are used to acquire such equipment, the Working Group recommends that LEAs give careful consideration to the appropriateness of acquiring such equipment for their communities and the appropriate use of such items in law enforcement actions.

a. Prohibited Equipment List

The Prohibited Equipment List serves to identify equipment that should not be authorized for LEAs to acquire via transfer from Federal agencies or purchase using Federally-provided funds.

RECOMMENDATION 1.1 — PROHIBITED EQUIPMENT LIST:

- **Tracked Armored Vehicles:** Vehicles that provide ballistic protection to their occupants and utilize a tracked system instead of wheels for forward motion.

- **Weaponized Aircraft, Vessels, and Vehicles of Any Kind:** These items will be prohibited from purchase or transfer with weapons installed.

- **Firearms of .50-Caliber or Higher**

- **Ammunition of .50-Caliber or Higher**

- **Grenade Launchers:** Firearm or firearm accessory designed to launch small explosive projectiles.

---

[20] The definitions on the equipment lists capture categories of equipment and, therefore, may be broader than specific item descriptions on existing authorized equipment lists. In implementing these recommendations, Federal agencies will provide guidance on which equipment falls under the defined categories of the Prohibited and Controlled Equipment Lists.

- **Bayonets:**   Large knives designed to be attached to the muzzle of a rifle/shotgun/long gun for the purposes of hand-to-hand combat.

- **Camouflage Uniforms:** Does not include woodland or desert patterns or solid color uniforms.

The Working Group concluded that a prohibition on acquisition of such equipment by LEAs from Federal programs is appropriate because the substantial risk of misusing or overusing these items, which are seen as militaristic in nature, could significantly undermine community trust and may encourage tactics and behaviors that are inconsistent with the premise of civilian law enforcement. These concerns outweigh the Federal Government's interest in providing this equipment to address law enforcement needs (that could not otherwise be fulfilled).

For example, although grenade launchers can be used to launch tear gas and other nonexplosive and less-than-lethal projectiles, their use and misuse can be detrimental to maintaining public trust in law enforcement,[21] and other devices that do not have similar militaristic connotations are available to launch tear gas. Camouflage-patterned uniforms are another example of equipment that is closely associated with the military. Certain types of camouflage patterns may be required for specific law enforcement missions conducted within a specific physical terrain and environment (such as woodland camouflage in forest areas for narcotic eradication programs) and therefore would be available through Federal programs. However, the acquisition of camouflage-patterned uniforms is not authorized where it will be used in environments, including urban settings, where they do not actually camouflage the wearer. Solid-color utility uniforms are not listed on the Prohibited or Controlled Equipment Lists and may continue to be acquired through Federal programs.

Similarly, although bayonets at one time were transferred under the 1033 program and can currently be purchased under some Federal grant programs, this type of equipment is likewise seen as incompatible with the concept of civilian law enforcement, particularly when other equipment, such as a utility knife, could be used for ordinary and other legitimate law enforcement purposes. Firearms of or over .50-caliber (and applicable ammunition) are also on the Prohibited Equipment List because this type of firearm, which is typically used for military operations, is very destructive and capable of penetrating structures and lightly armored vehicles. Tracked armored vehicles are included on the Prohibited Equipment List because they are designed specifically for use in military operations, their appearance may undermine community trust when used in support of civilian law enforcement activities, and LEAs can find alternative equipment options.[22]

---

[21] http://www.pewtrusts.org/en/research-and-analysis/blogs/stateline/2015/3/24/can-states-slow-the-flow-of-military-equipment-to-police.

[22] A Government-wide assessment is currently being conducted to identify the LEAs that have acquired the types of equipment identified on the recommended prohibited equipment list and determine whether individual agency authorities authorize a recall of the equipment.

b. Controlled Equipment List

Equipment identified on the Controlled Equipment List has significant utility for State, local, or Tribal law enforcement operations, and LEAs, other than those solely serving schools with grades ranging from kindergarten through grade 12,[23] may continue to acquire it through Federal programs. However, because of the lethal nature of the equipment and/or the potential negative impact on the community, LEAs are required to take additional steps to acquire this equipment, including the submission of a detailed justification outlining their need for procuring the equipment and certification that agency controls, such as the training and equipment use policies and procedures described below, are in place to prevent misuse of the equipment.

RECOMMENDATION 1.2 — CONTROLLED EQUIPMENT LIST:

- **Manned Aircraft, Fixed Wing:** Powered aircraft with a crew aboard, such as airplanes, that use a fixed wing for lift.

- **Manned Aircraft, Rotary Wing:** Powered aircraft with a crew aboard, such as helicopters, that use a rotary wing for lift.

- **Unmanned Aerial Vehicles:** A remotely piloted, powered aircraft without a crew aboard.

- **Armored Vehicles, Wheeled:** Any wheeled vehicle either purpose-built or modified to provide ballistic protection to its occupants, such as a Mine-Resistant Ambush Protected (MRAP) vehicle or an Armored Personnel Carrier. These vehicles are sometimes used by law enforcement personnel involved in dangerous operating conditions, including active shooter or similar high-threat situations. These vehicles often have weapon-firing ports.

- **Tactical Vehicles, Wheeled:** A vehicle purpose-built to operate on- and off-road in support of military operations, such as a HMMWV ("Humvee"), 2.5-ton truck, 5-ton truck, or a vehicle with a breaching or entry apparatus attached. These vehicles are sometimes used by law enforcement in rough terrain or inclement weather for search and rescue operations, as well as other law enforcement functions.

- **Command and Control Vehicles:** Any wheeled vehicle either purpose-built or modified to facilitate the operational control and direction of public safety units responding to an incident. Command and Control vehicles provide a

---

[23] The Permanent Working Group (see Recommendation 5.1), in consultation with higher education leaders, organizations, including campus law enforcement organizations, will further consider the extent to which acquisition of controlled equipment via Federal programs by LEAs operated by institutions of higher education furthers the interests of student and campus safety. If the PWG determines that such acquisition is appropriate in particular circumstances, then the PWG will establish standards and criteria, including a detailed explanation of the need for such equipment in the school or campus environment, to inform consideration of requests for, and appropriate use of, controlled equipment by LEAs operated by institutions of higher education.

variety of capabilities to the incident Commander, including, but not limited to, the provision for enhanced communications and other situational awareness capabilities.

- **Specialized Firearms and Ammunition Under .50-Caliber (excludes firearms and ammunition for service-issued weapons):** Weapons and corresponding ammunition for specialized operations or assignment. This excludes service-issued handguns, rifles, or shotguns that are issued or approved by the agency to be used during the course of regularly assigned duties.

- **Explosives and Pyrotechnics:** Includes "flash bangs" as well as explosive breaching tools often used by special operations units.

- **Breaching Apparatus (e.g. battering ram or similar entry device):** Tools designed to provide law enforcement rapid entry into a building or through a secured doorway. These tools may be mechanical in nature (a battering ram), ballistic (slugs), or explosive.

- **Riot Batons (excluding service-issued telescopic or fixed-length straight batons):** Non-expandable baton of greater length (generally in excess of 24 inches) than service-issued types and are intended to protect its wielder during melees by providing distance from assailants.

- **Riot Helmets:** Helmets designed to protect the wearer's face and head from injury during melees from projectiles including rocks, bricks, liquids, etc. Riot helmets include a visor which protects the face.

- **Riot Shields:** Shields intended to protect wielders from their head to their knees in melees. Most are designed for the protection of the user from projectiles including rocks, bricks, and liquids. Some afford limited ballistic protection as well. Riot shields may also be used as an offensive weapon to push opponents.

Equipment categories are included on the Controlled Equipment List for several reasons. Some categories describe equipment that could be seen as militaristic in nature yet also may have significant utility for law enforcement operations. This includes several types of armored vehicles, such as MRAP vehicles transferred via the 1033 program and armored vehicles manufactured commercially. These vehicles can provide critical officer and civilian safety protection and transport into and out of high-risk situations and therefore should not be prohibited. However, given the potential for misapplication of controlled equipment listed above, LEAs must provide expanded justification for its acquisition, including a description of how the equipment would be deployed, the agency's policies and protocols on deployment, and verification of training provided to LEAs on the appropriate use of such controlled equipment.

Other equipment categories on the Controlled Equipment List – e.g. Fixed Wing Aircraft, Rotary Wing Aircraft, Command and Control Vehicles – are included because they require special licenses to operate or their sheer size can have an undesired intimidating effect on the general public if used inappropriately or indiscriminately. Firearms and associated ammunition (under .50-caliber) used in special operations, that are outside of the normal service-issued handguns, rifles, and shotguns are also listed on the Controlled Equipment List, as is a subset of equipment that is typically utilized by special operations teams. The Working Group carefully considered the potential impact of this recommendation on officer safety and placed a high priority on providing law enforcement officers with access to equipment that would protect them in dangerous and violent situations. As such, service-issued handguns, rifles, and shotguns used for non-specialized activities and bulletproof vests and other body armor may be acquired using Federal resources according to existing program parameters. For riot control equipment, LEAs may acquire it after certifying that the LEA meets the additional requirements described below and have received approval from the Federal equipment acquisition program.

* * * * *

The Prohibited Equipment List will take effect upon transmission of the recommendations to the President. The remaining recommendations below will be implemented not later than the beginning of Fiscal Year 2016 (October 1, 2015). Federal agencies will notify current and prospective controlled equipment applicants about changes to the acquisition programs and will issue guidance documents and conduct trainings on these developments.

It should be noted that unless otherwise indicated, the following recommendations on policies, training, acquisitions, and transfers and sales to third parties apply to all items on the Controlled Equipment List. Additionally, these requirements are triggered only when an LEA acquires controlled equipment using Federal resources beginning in Fiscal Year 2016. In other words, if an LEA opts to participate in Federal controlled equipment acquisitions programs on or after October 1, 2015, the changes to the programs that are reflected in these recommendations will apply, unless otherwise indicated.

* * * * *

2. POLICIES, TRAINING, AND PROTOCOLS FOR CONTROLLED EQUIPMENT

> *Develop policies to ensure that LEAs abide by any limitations or affirmative obligations imposed on the acquisition of controlled equipment or receipt of funds to purchase controlled equipment from the Federal Government and the obligations resulting from receipt of Federal financial assistance.*
>
> *Executive Order 13688, Section 3(v)*

> *Require that LEAs participating in Federal controlled equipment programs receive necessary training regarding appropriate use of controlled equipment and the implementation of obligations resulting from receipt of Federal financial assistance, including training on the protection of civil rights and civil liberties.*
>
> *Executive Order 13688, Section 3(ix)*

> *Require after-action analysis reports for significant incidents involving federally provided or federally funded controlled equipment.*
>
> *Executive Order 13688, Section 3(iv)*

To demonstrate that controlled equipment is used in a way that keeps their communities safe while also protecting the rights of community members, LEAs must adopt robust and specific policies and protocols governing appropriate, constitutionally-sound uses of controlled equipment. Training on these protocols and policies also is essential so that LEA personnel are fully aware of their agency's expectations, operations, and restrictions with respect to general policing as well as the use of controlled equipment. LEAs should regularly review how they are using controlled equipment and whether the use of that equipment continues to be necessary and appropriate.

Many LEAs already have substantial policies and training requirements in place. The District of Columbia's Metropolitan Police Department (MPD) Academy, for example, instructs recruit officers on subjects such as the laws of arrest, search and seizure, criminal law, traffic regulations, human relations, community policing, ethics, operation of emergency police vehicles, self-defense, and advanced first aid. The University of Texas System Police (UTSP) has a policy on Emergency Rescue Armored Personnel Vehicle (MRAP), which specifies that the "exclusive operational purpose" of the MRAP is to enhance the physical protection of its occupants. Accordingly, the policy requires that any MRAP vehicle display the words "Emergency Rescue," so that its purpose is clear to the community. Further, unless the Police Director expressly authorizes use of the MRAP in response to other specified emergency circumstances (e.g., an active shooter), the UTSP policy explicitly prohibits the use of MRAP vehicles in response to "exercises of the First Amendment right to free speech" or as a part of "any public demonstration or display of police resources." The USTP policy also requires the police academy to develop training consistent with the vehicle's mission for officers who are most likely to utilize the vehicle, with such training including, at a minimum, "engagement and deployment with this vehicle as well as use of the vehicle to successfully and safely rescue those requiring evacuation."

However, some LEAs may not have the necessary policies and training mechanisms in place for a variety of reasons – including unfamiliarity with examples of relevant policies, reliance on informal training methods, cost limitations, lack of training options, or an assumption that such explicit policies and training for controlled equipment are not necessary. An additional challenge to developing consistent nationwide training for controlled equipment for LEAs is that, both in-service and academy-based training may be procured or provided through a number of different sources. Some LEAs conduct their own training while others rely on state or regional training boards or some combination of these.

With these considerations in mind, the Working Group developed a series of recommendations that would require minimum standards for policy development, training, and the review of the use of controlled equipment. LEAs are encouraged to go beyond these minimum standards and adopt promising practices that can be shared through communities of practice. In adopting, revising, or amplifying policies and training related to controlled equipment use, community input and impact must be meaningfully considered. The Federal Government will support these local efforts by working with law enforcement, civil rights and community groups, and academics to develop resources such as model policies or training modules that can be replicated and applied locally.

a. Policies and Protocols

Under this Recommendation, LEA policies must include protocols on general policing principles as well as specific protocols on the appropriate use of controlled equipment. Both components are critical and complementary. At the outset, there must be an agency-wide commitment to partner with the community the LEA is sworn to protect and serve, to respect and uphold community members' civil rights and civil liberties, and to receive the public's input regarding the LEA's activities in a meaningful way. As a result of that commitment and engagement, LEAs can develop specific policies and protocols to determine, among other things, when, how often, and in what manner controlled equipment should be used.

RECOMMENDATION 2.1 — POLICIES AND PROTOCOLS: LEAs that acquire controlled equipment through Federal programs must adopt robust and specific written policies and protocols governing General Policing Standards and Specific Controlled Equipment Standards.

- **General Policing Standards** includes policies on (a) Community Policing; (b) Constitutional Policing; and (c) Community Input and Impact Considerations.

- **Specific Controlled Equipment Standards** includes policies specifically related to (a) Appropriate Use of Controlled Equipment; (b) Supervision of Use; (c) Effectiveness Evaluation; (d) Auditing and Accountability; and (e) Transparency and Notice Considerations.

- **Record-Keeping Requirement.** Upon request, LEAs must provide a copy of the General Policing Standards and Specific Controlled Equipment Standards, and any related policies and protocols, to the Federal agency that supplied the equipment/funds.

Recommendation 2.1 is designed to incorporate relevant policies and protocols into the LEA's organizational or strategic plan that defines the agency's mission, goals, and objectives and informs its operational and technical needs. The General Policing Standards, therefore, delineate three essential policy issues that apply to all aspects of an LEA's mission and function:

- *Community Policing* is the concept that trust and mutual respect between police and the communities they serve are critical to public safety. Community policing fosters relationships between law enforcement and the local community which promotes public confidence in LEAs and, in turn, enhances LEAs ability to investigate crimes and keep the peace.

- *Constitutional Policing* protocols emphasize that all police work should be carried out in a manner consistent with the requirements of the U.S. Constitution and federal law. Policies must include protocols on First Amendment, Fourth Amendment, and Fourteenth Amendment principles in law enforcement activity, as well as compliance with Federal and State civil rights laws.[24]

- *Community Input and Impact* protocols must identify mechanisms that LEAs will use to engage the communities they serve to inform them and seek their input about LEAs' actions, role in, and relationships with the community. Law enforcement exists to protect and serve the community, so it is axiomatic that the community should be aware of and have a say in how they are policed. LEAs should make particular efforts to seek the input of communities where controlled equipment is likely to be used so as to mitigate the effect that such use may have on public confidence in the police. This could be achieved through the LEA's regular interactions with the public through community forums, town halls, or meetings with the Chief or community outreach divisions.

The LEA's General Policing Standards should inform protocols on the five components of the Specific Controlled Equipment Standards.

- *Appropriate Use of Controlled Equipment.* The protocols must define appropriate use of controlled equipment. LEAs should examine scenarios in which controlled equipment will likely be deployed, the decision-making processes that will determine whether controlled equipment is used, and the potential that both use and misuse of controlled equipment could create fear and distrust in the community. Protocols should consider whether

---

[24] This includes, among others, Title VI of the Civil Rights Act, the Omnibus Crime Control and Safe Streets Act, Deprivation of Rights Under Color of Law (18 U.S.C. § 242), Conspiracy Against Rights (18 U.S.C. § 241), 42 U.S.C. 1983, and 42 U.S.C. 14141.

measures can be taken to mitigate that effect (e.g., keep armored vehicles at a staging area until needed) and any alternatives to the use of such equipment and tactics to minimize negative effects on the community, while preserving officer safety.

- *Supervision of Use.* The protocols must specify appropriate supervision of personnel operating or utilizing controlled equipment. Supervision must be tailored to the type of equipment being used and the nature of the engagement or operation during which the equipment will be used. Policies must describe when a supervisor of appropriate authority is required to be present and actively overseeing the equipment's use in the field.

- *Effectiveness Evaluation.* The protocols must articulate that the LEA will regularly monitor and evaluate the effectiveness and value of controlled equipment to determine whether continued deployment and use is warranted on operational, tactical, and technical grounds. LEAs should routinely review after-action reports and analyze any data on, for example, how often controlled equipment is used or whether controlled equipment is used more frequently in certain law enforcement operations or in particular locations or neighborhoods.

- *Auditing and Accountability.* There must be strong auditing and accountability provisions in the protocols which state that LEA personnel will agree to and comply with and be held accountable if they do not adhere to agency, State, local, Tribal, and Federal policies associated with the use of controlled equipment.

- *Transparency and Notice.* The protocols must articulate that LEAs will engage the community regarding acquisition of controlled equipment, policies governing its use, and review of Significant Incidents (see Recommendation 2.3 below), with the understanding that there are reasonable limitations on disclosures of certain information and law enforcement sensitive operations and procedures.

Before a Federal agency transfers any controlled equipment to an LEA or provides approval for an LEA to use Federal funds to acquire controlled equipment, the LEA must certify that it has adopted General Policing Standards and Specific Controlled Equipment Standards, which will be defined further in subsequent Federal agency guidance. DOJ also will partner with law enforcement, civil rights, and civil liberties stakeholder groups to make available model policies and protocols related to the General Policing and Specific Controlled Equipment Standards for use by LEAs.

b. Training

Appropriate and relevant training for LEA personnel on General Policing Standards, Specific Controlled Equipment Standards, and the technical operation of controlled equipment is vital to fully implementing LEA policies and protocols and to ensuring that the use of controlled equipment complies with constitutional standards for the protection of civil rights and civil liberties. Training objectives should define and explain relevant concepts and demonstrate the application of such concepts through equipment-based scenarios to show appropriate and proper use of controlled equipment by law enforcement personnel and the negative effects and consequences of misuse.

RECOMMENDATION 2.2 — TRAINING: LEAs that acquire controlled equipment through Federal programs must ensure that its personnel are appropriately trained and that training meets the following requirements:

- **Required Annual Training on Protocols.** On an annual basis, all LEA personnel who may use or authorize use of controlled equipment must be trained on the LEA's General Policing Standards and Specific Controlled Equipment Standards.

- **Required Operational and Technical Training.** LEA personnel who use controlled equipment must be properly trained on, and have achieved technical proficiency in, the operation or utilization of the controlled equipment at issue.

- **Scenario-Based Training.** To the extent possible, LEA trainings related to controlled equipment should include scenario-based training that combines constitutional and community policing principles with equipment-specific training. LEA personnel authorizing or directing the use of controlled equipment should have enhanced scenario-based training to examine, deliberate, and review the circumstances in which controlled equipment should or should not be used.

- **Record-Keeping Requirement.** LEAs must retain comprehensive training records, either in the personnel file of the officer who was trained or by the LEA's training division or equivalent entity, for a period of at least three (3) years, and must provide a copy of these records, upon request, to the Federal agency that supplied the equipment/funds.

The requirements in Recommendation 2.2 are designed to complement existing LEA training that accomplishes similar purposes. For example, LEAs that currently have robust policies on community policing, civil rights and civil liberties, and community input and impact, and train personnel on those policies, may already be able to meet the General Policing Standards training requirement if the training is provided annually. Typically, these subjects are part of training for new recruits at police academies and during annual in-services on agency-wide policies and procedures, updates to the law and legal standards, and emerging issues and techniques. LEAs should review the training they currently provide to determine whether it aligns with the General Policing Standards.

Training is also widely available on the technical operation of some controlled equipment. For officers assigned to special operations teams, LEAs often provide training on and require proficiency in operating specialized firearms and vehicles as well as tactics and procedures. And LEA personnel who fly Fixed or Rotary Wing Aircraft are required to maintain all applicable licensing requirements.

Training on Specific Controlled Equipment Standards, however, may not be as comprehensive or as prevalent among LEAs as is necessary to ensure proper use of controlled equipment. To assist LEAs, Federal agencies, including DOJ's Office of Justice Programs, will partner with relevant stakeholders to develop and produce training programs, and disseminate existing training curricula, to address the appropriate use of controlled equipment and related topics.

c. After-Action Review

LEAs, the communities they serve, and the Federal Government all have an interest in ensuring that when LEAs acquire controlled equipment they use that equipment appropriately – consistent with the protocols they have adopted and the training they provide to their personnel. Whether an LEA uses controlled equipment appropriately and according to required protocols and training also is a key factor in determining its eligibility for continued or future participation in Federal controlled equipment acquisition programs.

In order to determine whether LEAs' use of controlled equipment is consistent with their protocols and training, interested parties must be able to review information describing whether, how, and in what circumstances the controlled equipment was used. One significant step that would provide insight into an LEA's controlled equipment use practices is requiring LEAs to collect and retain certain information on the use of controlled equipment. When combined with the LEA's adoption of requisite protocols and provision of mandatory training, this data will increase transparency for communities and lay the foundation for robust accountability and federal oversight when controlled equipment is used. The recommendations set forth below balance the need for this information against the potential burden placed on LEAs to collect and retain this data. Thus, the recommendation takes into account common existing LEA reporting and documentation practices in order to avoid duplication or other costly and time-intensive efforts.

RECOMMENDATION 2.3 — AFTER-ACTION REVIEW: (1) LEAs must collect and retain "Required Information" (described below) when law enforcement activity that involves a "Significant Incident" requires, or results in, the use of any Federally-acquired controlled equipment in the LEA's inventory (or any other controlled equipment in the same category as the Federally-acquired controlled equipment). (2) When unlawful or inappropriate police actions are alleged and trigger a Federal compliance review, and the Federal agency determines that controlled or prohibited equipment was used in the law enforcement activity under review, the LEA must produce or generate a report(s) containing Required Information.

- **"Significant Incident" Defined:** Any law enforcement operation or action that involves (a) a violent encounter among civilians or between civilians and the police; (b) a use-of-force that causes death or serious bodily injury[25]; (c) a demonstration or other public exercise of First Amendment rights; or (d) an event that draws, or could be reasonably expected to draw, a large number of attendees or participants, such as those where advanced planning is needed.

- **"Required Information" to Be Collected and Retained:** (a) Identification of controlled equipment used (e.g., categories and number of units of controlled equipment used, make/model/serial number); (b) description of the law enforcement operation involving the controlled equipment; (c) identification of LEA personnel who used the equipment and, if possible, civilians involved in the incident; and (d) result of controlled equipment use (e.g., arrests, use-of-force, victim extraction, injuries).

- **Format of Information Collection and Retention.** No new form or format is required as long as the Required Information is retained in a manner that is easily accessible and organized. For example, information about the use of controlled equipment can be included in an Operations Plan, detailed in officer daily logs, or described in use-of-force reports.

- **Record-Keeping Requirement.** LEAs must retain "Significant Incident" reports and Required Information for a period of at least three (3) years and must provide a copy of these records, upon request, to the Federal agency that supplied the equipment/funds. This information also should be made available to the community the LEA serves in accordance with applicable policies and protocols including considerations regarding the disclosure of sensitive information.

This recommendation focuses first on information collection and retention for LEA controlled equipment use in major events and incidents that affect a larger segment of the community. The definition of "Significant Incident," therefore, captures actual or planned uses of controlled equipment for events involving a large number of people or those that would garner public attention or inquiry because of the nature of what transpired. The second part of the recommendation requires the collection or production of information for incidents that may not be as public but still could have a significant effect on the police-community relationship. Not every complaint or allegation of inappropriate police action would prompt the generation or production of information; rather, only those where a Federal agency determines a compliance review or investigation is merited would compel such additional action.

The recommendation identifies a limited number of categories of information that must be collected and retained when controlled equipment is used. First, LEAs must identify the particular piece(s) of controlled equipment used. LEAs can achieve this by documenting, for example, the type of equipment and serial number or other unique marking of individual items.

---

[25] See 18 U.S.C. § 1365(h)(3): "[T]he term 'serious bodily injury' means bodily injury which involves (A) a substantial risk of death; (B) extreme physical pain; (C) protracted and obvious disfigurement; or (D) protracted loss or impairment of the function of a bodily member, organ, or mental faculty."

Second, in describing the law enforcement operation requiring controlled equipment, LEAs must include commonly documented information such as date, time, and location of the operation; the purpose of the operation; and whether the operation involved a specialized unit. Third, LEAs must identify the officer or agent who used and directed the use of the controlled equipment and also identify or describe civilians who were the subject or target of the investigation or action. For large crowds or multiple persons, the recommendation contemplates a general description of the civilians (e.g., "a crowd of approximately 250 people"). Finally, the result of the operation also should be documented, including any arrests or citations, injuries or fatalities (involving officers or civilians), uses-of force, victim extraction, or property damage.

Many of the Required Information categories are likely to be documented already in existing police reports that are generated for Significant Incidents. For example, if a large demonstration is anticipated, it is common for an LEA to prepare an Operations Plan, which likely will include, at a minimum, a description of the anticipated demonstration, the LEA personnel who will respond, the number of civilians that are likely to attend, and any special equipment that will be used. The LEA also will likely produce other forms as a matter of course after the Significant Incident takes place, such as incident, arrest, or use-of-force reports, if applicable. And many LEAs routinely complete an After-Action Report following a large demonstration or event that evaluates the operation and effectiveness of the LEA response. In these situations, the LEA must simply ensure that the Operations Plan or other related report includes information that controlled equipment was used. No new form or format is required as long as the Required Information is retained in a manner that is easily accessible and organized.

LEAs that acquire controlled equipment through Federal programs on or after October 1, 2015, must collect and retain Required Information for any controlled equipment in their inventory, regardless of when they acquired it, as long as one unit of equipment in that category was acquired using Federal resources. For example, an LEA acquires a Fixed Wing Aircraft in FY16 through a Federal program and had acquired a Tactical Vehicle in FY15 through a Federal program. If these are the only Federally-acquired controlled equipment in the LEA's inventory, the LEA must collect and retain Required Information for all Fixed Wing Aircraft and all Tactical Vehicles in its inventory. The LEA is not required to collect and retain Required Information for any other controlled equipment in its inventory that was acquired using only non-Federal sources.

The recommendation does not include a requirement to provide regular reports to the Federal Government. Instead, LEAs only are required to collect and retain this information and provide it to the Federal Government upon request. As the recommendation states, Federal agencies will request this information when they conduct compliance reviews or investigations triggered by a complaint or an incident for inappropriate or unlawful law enforcement actions. Federal agencies may also request this information to evaluate an LEA's future applications for controlled equipment or when they conduct regular or periodic compliance reviews to assess the program participant's progress toward stated project goals and to ensure programmatic and administrative compliance.

This information also should be made available to the community the LEA serves in accordance with the LEA's General Policing Standards, Specific Controlled Equipment Standards, and other applicable policies and protocols including considerations regarding the disclosure of sensitive information. While the recommendation requires LEAs to collect and retain information and data under the prescribed circumstances described above, LEAs are encouraged to work with their communities to expand the type of information that is collected and to determine how best to share that information with relevant stakeholders. In all, the information collected and retained under this recommendation has considerable potential to improve transparency between LEAs and the communities they serve, ultimately providing community members with a greater awareness and understanding of police actions and giving law enforcement leaders additional opportunities for community engagement.

3. ACQUISITION PROCESS FOR CONTROLLED EQUIPMENT

> *Harmonize Federal programs so that they have consistent and transparent policies with respect to the acquisition of controlled equipment by LEAs.*
>
> Executive Order 13688, Section 3(iii)

> *Require local civilian government (non-police) review of and authorization for LEAs' request for or acquisition of controlled equipment.*
>
> Executive Order 13688, Section 3(viii)

Each of the Federal programs that provide LEAs with controlled equipment or the resources to purchase it has unique requirements based on its authorizing legislation. Some programs, such as DOD's 1033 program, were created expressly for the purpose of providing equipment to LEAs. Others, such as DOJ's Byrne JAG program, are formula grants to State, local, and Tribal agencies that support a range of law enforcement and criminal justice priorities. Because of the varying purposes of these acquisition programs, inconsistencies exist among Federal agencies in the type and amount of information they require of LEAs in order to acquire controlled equipment. For example, only three agencies currently require information related to the size of the requesting LEA or the population of the LEA's jurisdiction. Just two agencies require evidence of a training plan as a part of the criteria. And only four agencies require information on the availability of requested equipment that is either already in the possession of the requesting LEA or is available via applicable mutual aid agreements.

Harmonizing Federal program requirements to the extent possible will contribute to greater continuity and commonality across the Federal Government and provide LEAs with a better understanding of equipment acquisition processes, regardless of the Federal program. Standardized criteria also will enhance collaboration among programs, allowing Federal agencies to evaluate LEA applications for controlled equipment more thoroughly and to make decisions in a more informed and consistent manner.

RECOMMENDATION 3.1 — APPLICATION INFORMATION: In addition to application requirements mandated by individual Federal acquisitions programs, LEAs must submit information in the following categories for approval in all requests for controlled equipment:

- General description of the LEA.

- Detailed justification for acquiring the controlled equipment, including a clear and persuasive explanation of the need for the equipment and the appropriate law enforcement purpose that it will serve. An LEA's application for controlled equipment should describe any previous instance in which the controlled equipment was used in a manner that deviated from the detailed justification supporting the application for that equipment.

- Number of units of the requested controlled equipment that the LEA currently has in its inventory.

- Categories of other controlled equipment acquired through Federal programs during the past three (3) years that the LEA currently has in its inventory.

- Whether the requested controlled equipment currently could reasonably be accessed through loans or mutual assistance or mutual aid agreements.

- Certification that the LEA has adopted required protocols (see Recommendation 2.1) or will adopt those protocols <u>before</u> physical acquisition or purchase of controlled equipment or transfer of funds.

- Certification that the LEA has provided required training (see Recommendation 2.2) or will provide that training <u>before</u> physical acquisition or purchase of controlled equipment or transfer of funds.

- Evidence of civilian governing body's review and approval or concurrence of the LEA's acquisition of the requested controlled equipment.[26]

- Whether the requesting LEA has applied, or has a pending application(s), for this type of controlled equipment from another Federal agency during the current fiscal year.

- Whether any prior application for controlled equipment has been denied by a Federal agency during the past three (3) years, and, if so, the reason for the denial.

- Whether the LEA has been found to be in violation of a Federal civil rights statute or programmatic term during the past three (3) years and, if so, whether any disposition was reached or corrective actions were taken.

---

[26] For purposes of this criteria, a "governing body" is defined as the institution or organization that has direct budgetary oversight or fiscal/financial control over the requesting LEA.

An applicant's compliance with the requirements described in Recommendation 3.1 will provide program decision-makers with a clearer understanding of an LEA's capacity and need for using the controlled equipment. These criteria will be incorporated into each Federal acquisition program's existing application processes. LEAs will be required to certify that their responses are accurate, to the best of their knowledge. Any knowing misrepresentations may be subject to a penalty, including criminal prosecution.

The first criterion requires requesting LEAs to provide a description and size of the LEA including the number of sworn full-time and part-time law enforcement officers and the population of the jurisdiction served by the agency. There is no size or population threshold that the LEA has to meet in order to participate in Federal equipment acquisition programs; rather, this information provides the Federal acquisition program with a general picture of the capacity and need of the LEA.

LEAs also will be required to articulate a detailed justification for acquiring the controlled equipment. Controlled equipment will not be appropriate for every LEA. Applications for controlled equipment should not be granted in the absence of a clear and persuasive explanation of the need for the equipment and the appropriate law enforcement purpose that it will serve. Such explanation should specifically address the current needs of the community and the resources already available to the LEA to serve those needs. It is expected that LEA rationales will involve some degree of contingency planning and will vary in their level of detail depending on the individual Federal acquisition program's authorization and purpose. Nevertheless, LEAs should not be vague in articulating this justification by resorting to general notions of preparedness – and should anticipate that the application will be carefully evaluated by the relevant Federal agency to determine whether it is sufficient. As described below, there will be ongoing coordination among the various Federal agencies to ensure that a uniform process is in place to assess the adequacy of the justification in each application.

As part of the application process, Federal agencies also will require LEAs to describe the current availability of controlled equipment to the LEA, primarily to assess the LEA's need for the requested equipment. The LEA must provide the number of units of the requested item that are currently in the LEA's inventory (e.g., the number of aircraft in the LEA's fleet) and all categories of controlled equipment acquired through Federal programs for the past three (3) years. The LEA also must indicate whether the requested controlled equipment currently is available through loans, mutual assistance agreements, or mutual aid agreements. Important in this evaluation is a description of the equipment to which the LEA has access, including its age and functionality. The sufficiency of the LEA's current access to controlled equipment, or viable alternative to such equipment, should inform the assessment of the application.

The requesting LEA must certify that it has adopted the General Policing Standards and the Specific Controlled Equipment Standards and provided training on these protocols. The requesting LEA must also certify that it has ensured that its personnel have been appropriately trained and have obtained the necessary licenses or similar authorizations to operate controlled equipment. If the LEA at the time of the application has not completed protocol or training requirements, it must certify that those requirements will be completed before the LEA takes possession of or purchases the controlled equipment or accepts funds from the relevant Federal agency.[27] The LEA may be required to provide the Federal agency that supplied the equipment/funds with copies of relevant protocols and training records.

Requesting LEAs must provide evidence of approval or concurrence by the jurisdiction's governing body (e.g., City Council, County Council, Mayor) for the acquisition of the requested controlled equipment. Evidence of the governing body's approval or concurrence should be explicit. But if the LEA can provide evidence that the governing body was given a reasonable opportunity to review the controlled equipment acquisition request but failed to affirmatively approve or disapprove of the request, such silence or inaction will constitute evidence of approval. This requirement applies to LEAs where the chief executive is an elected position (e.g., Sheriff and the governing body is the County Council). Requiring approval or concurrence by the governing body is a significant way to involve representatives of the community, through its elected leaders, in the decision to add controlled equipment to an LEA's inventory and to use it in the jurisdiction.

The recommendation also requires the requesting LEA to self-report if it has applied for this type of controlled equipment from another Federal agency during the current fiscal year, including any pending applications, or has been denied controlled equipment by a Federal agency during the past three (3) years, and, if so, the reason for the denial. LEAs must also disclose instances in which the controlled equipment deviated from the detailed justification supporting the application for that equipment. The LEA must also disclose whether it has been found to be in violation of any Federal civil rights criminal or civil statute or programmatic term or condition during the past three (3) years. If so, the LEA should provide a description of the findings and whether any disposition was reached or corrective actions were undertaken.

RECOMMENDATION 3.2 — REGIONAL SHARING: The requesting LEA must indicate whether the requested controlled equipment is being acquired to provide a regional or multijurisdictional capability. In such cases, requesting LEAs must:

- Provide information regarding the size of the region, including the number and size of the LEA with access to the requested controlled equipment and the estimated population served.

- Certify that all LEAs in the regional sharing arrangement have adopted requisite protocols (see Recommendation 2.1) or will adopt those protocols before their personnel use the controlled equipment.

---

[27] In circumstances in which LEA possession of the controlled equipment is necessary for technical or operational training because similar equipment is otherwise unavailable for training purposes, the LEA may certify that it will provide such technical and operational training prior to the use of the controlled equipment.

- Certify that all LEAs in the regional sharing arrangement have provided requisite training (see Recommendation 2.2) or will provide that training <u>before</u> their personnel use the controlled equipment.

- Certify that all LEAs in the regional sharing arrangement will adhere to the information collection and retention requirements (see Recommendation 2.3).

LEAs may want to acquire certain controlled equipment – due to size, cost, scarcity, or other reason – for use in regional sharing arrangements, and the Working Group strongly encourages such arrangements. In those situations, jurisdictions typically enter into a Memorandum of Understanding or other agreement that describes the parameters of use and how the equipment will be shared among the participating LEAs. If an LEA is requesting controlled equipment for regional sharing purposes, it must notify the Federal agency in its application and provide relevant information on each participating LEA. Likewise, if an LEA decides after acquisition to make such equipment available to other LEAs in a regional sharing arrangement, it must notify the Federal agency that supplied or funded the equipment. The relevant information includes the size of each participating LEA and jurisdiction and certifications that each participating LEA, and any subsequent participating LEA, will fulfill the same protocols, training, and information collection and retention requirements as the requesting LEA. Importantly, the requesting LEA, unless expressly provided otherwise, will be the primary agency responsible for the acquired controlled equipment and will be the agency held accountable and subject to sanctions for any programmatic violations by participating agencies.

4. TRANSFER, SALE, RETURN, AND DISPOSAL OF CONTROLLED EQUIPMENT

Ensure a process for returning specified controlled equipment that was acquired from the Federal Government when no longer needed by an LEA.

Executive Order 13688, Section 3(vii)

Create a process to monitor the sale or transfer of controlled equipment from the Federal Government or controlled equipment purchased with funds from the Federal Government by LEAs to third parties.

Executive Order 13688, Section 3(xi)

When an LEA divests itself of controlled equipment, it is incumbent upon the LEA to transfer, sell, return, or dispose of the equipment in a safe, conscientious manner that takes into account hazards or risks if used by others in the future. The type of equipment that will be transferred or sold is an important factor in assessing the level of risk when used by a third party. As noted above, some categories of equipment are included on the Controlled Equipment List due to the potential harmful effect on the community if used inappropriately by law enforcement; those harms may not exist outside of the policing context. Other items carry significant inherent safety risks, especially if they are not handled by trained law enforcement officers.

Federal agencies currently impose few if any conditions or restrictions on how LEAs transfer or sell controlled equipment to third parties, with the exception of GSA rules governing the donation of equipment and DOD which retains title to equipment provided through its 1033 program and already has in place robust and explicit requirements for the return of that equipment. The recommendations below provide uniform standards to which all Federal agencies and LEAs must adhere when transferring, selling, returning, or disposing of controlled equipment.

RECOMMENDATION 4.1 — TRANSFER/SALE OF CONTROLLED EQUIPMENT TO OTHER LEAs: LEAs may transfer or sell any controlled equipment, except riot helmets and shields, to another LEA. Prior to finalizing any transfer or sales agreement, the transferor/seller-LEA must inform and obtain approval from the Federal agency that supplied the controlled equipment/funds. The acquiring-LEA must submit the same information (see Recommendations 3.1, 3.2) that was required of the transferor/seller-LEA to, and receive approval from, the Federal agency.

RECOMMENDATION 4.2 — TRANSFER/SALE OF CONTROLLED EQUIPMENT TO NON-LEAs: LEAs may transfer or sell only the following types of controlled equipment to non-LEAs: (a) Fixed Wing Aircraft; (b) Rotary Wing Aircraft; and (c) Command And Control Vehicles. All law enforcement-related and other sensitive or potentially dangerous components, and all law enforcement insignias and identifying markings, must be removed prior to transfer or sale. The transferor/seller-LEA must inform and receive approval from the Federal agency from which the controlled equipment or funding to purchase the equipment was acquired prior to the finalization of any transfer or sale.

RECOMMENDATION 4.3 — RETURN OF CONTROLLED EQUIPMENT: LEAs that acquire controlled equipment through DOD's 1033 program must abide by its requirements governing the return and/or disposal of controlled equipment.

RECOMMENDATION 4.4 — DISPOSAL OF CONTROLLED EQUIPMENT: LEAs must abide by all applicable Federal, State, and local laws, regulations, and programmatic terms when disposing of controlled equipment. Prior to disposal, LEAs must notify the Federal agency that supplied the controlled equipment/funds.

Recommendation 4.1 requires LEAs who purchase or receive controlled equipment from another LEA that originally acquired the controlled equipment using Federal resources to adhere to the same protocols, training, and other requirements and obligations. This recommendation contemplates that the Federal and community interest in the appropriate use of controlled equipment continues to apply to subsequent acquiring-LEAs. The recommendation does not place any restriction on the type of equipment that can be transferred or sold to other LEAs, except riot control helmets and shields which cannot be transferred or sold at all because of the difficulty in providing assurances that they remain suitable for use as protective equipment. However, any third-party LEA purchasing or receiving controlled equipment acquired through a

Federal program must go through the same application and approval process as the LEA that initially acquired the controlled equipment.

Controls on the transfer or sale of controlled equipment to non-LEAs are determined based on the type of equipment involved. Explosives, firearms and ammunition, armored vehicles, and Unmanned Aerial Vehicles present potentially substantial risks if possessed and used by civilians. Recommendation 4.2 considers three items on the Controlled Equipment List – Fixed Wing Aircraft, Rotary Wing Aircraft, and Command and Control Vehicles – to be suitable for sale or transfer to the general public as long as any sensitive or law enforcement components and insignias are removed. In practical terms, this equipment without sensitive components and law enforcement markings are essentially airplanes, helicopters, and recreational vehicles (RVs) that can serve everyday commercial and private capacities.

Penalties for violation of such sales and transfers requirements will be applied if the applicable Federal agency subsequently learns of a sale or transfer in violation of such restrictions. Those violations would be considered programmatic, as addressed below.

5. OVERSIGHT, COMPLIANCE, AND IMPLEMENTATION

Establish a process to review and approve proposed additions or deletions to the list of controlled equipment.

Executive Order 13688, Section 3(ii)

Plan the creation of a database that includes information about controlled equipment purchased or acquired through Federal programs.

Executive Order 13688, Section 3(vi)

Provide uniform standards for suspending LEAs from Federal controlled equipment programs for specified violations of law, including civil rights laws, and ensuring those standards are implemented consistently across agencies.

Executive Order 13688, Section 3(x)

The Federal Government must take steps to ensure LEA compliance with controlled equipment acquisition, use, and disposal requirements. As part of implementing the recommendations, Federal agencies will conduct compliance reviews, consistent with the program's statutory or other authorities, focused on adherence to fiscal and programmatic terms and conditions including financial and programmatic obligations and adherence to civil rights statutes and requirements. Compliance reviews can range from requests for information to multiple on-site visits depending on the nature and the severity of the matter being reviewed. Similar to the variances in Federal acquisition processes, Federal agencies also have different methods and capabilities to conduct compliance reviews as well as varying terms and sanctions by program, which leads to inconsistent identification of and consequences for violations. As discussed below, the Permanent Working Group will ensure to the extent possible that there is consistency in the manner and process by which compliance reviews are conducted.

While compliance reviews and oversight are essential, the Federal Government also must provide incentives and opportunities to encourage law enforcement and communities to improve existing practices and adopt better practices. It also must improve Federal processes to increase efficiencies throughout Federal acquisitions programs. The recommendations below describe some of those efforts.

RECOMMENDATION 5.1 — PERMANENT LAW ENFORCEMENT EQUIPMENT WORKING GROUP: The members of the Working Group will form a permanent Federal Interagency Law Enforcement Equipment Working Group that meets regularly to support oversight and policy development functions for controlled equipment programs. The Permanent Working Group (PWG) will:

- Examine and evaluate the Controlled and Prohibited Equipment Lists for possible additions or deletions.

- Track LEA controlled equipment inventory.

- Ensure Government-wide criteria to evaluate requests for controlled equipment.

- Ensure uniform standards for compliance reviews.

- Track LEA sanctions and violations related to controlled equipment programs and usage.

RECOMMENDATION 5.2 — SANCTIONS FOR VIOLATIONS OF CONTROLLED EQUIPMENT PROGRAMS:

- **For Programmatic Violations.** For violations of any programmatic term or condition related to controlled equipment (e.g., failure to adopt required protocols, unauthorized transfers), the LEA will be suspended from acquiring additional controlled equipment through Federal programs for a minimum of 60 days. The suspension will continue until the Federal agency determines that the violation has been corrected. This does not prohibit a Federal agency from imposing other applicable sanctions according to applicable program parameters.

- **Statutory Violations.** For alleged violations of law, including civil rights laws, the matter will be referred for investigation to the Federal agency's Office of Civil Rights (OCR) or other appropriate compliance office, or the U.S. Department of Justice. If the investigation results in a finding that the LEA violated a civil rights or other relevant statute, the LEA will be sanctioned according to statute and/or the Federal agency's governing rules and policies. At a minimum, the LEA will be suspended from acquiring additional controlled equipment through Federal programs for a minimum of 60 days. The suspension will last until the Federal agency determines that the violation has been corrected.

The Permanent Working Group (PWG) will be responsible for the implementation of the recommendations in this report and will coordinate the policies of Federal equipment acquisitions programs. Specifically, the PWG will take on three important and related functions. First, the PWG will facilitate the sharing of relevant information among Federal agencies which will lead to greater harmonization of policies and the reduction of duplication and inconsistencies in agency operations. This includes:

- *Examine and evaluate the Controlled and Prohibited Equipment Lists for possible additions or deletions.* This periodic analysis will determine whether the Prohibited and Controlled Equipment Lists are up-to-date and reflect the development of new technologies or changes in patterns of usage. On an annual basis, the PWG will evaluate the items on the Controlled and Prohibited Equipment Lists and determine – with the input of relevant stakeholders – whether other types of equipment should be added to or deleted from these lists.

- *Track LEA inventory of controlled equipment.* Currently, only DOD has a comprehensive system to track equipment it has transferred to LEAs. For grant and other programs that provide LEAs with funds to purchase equipment, tracking equipment currently is more difficult because the LEA holds title to the equipment. Tracking controlled equipment will be easier with the implementation of the recommendations in this report – namely, the requirement that LEAs must receive approval from the Federal Government for transfers or sales of equipment to third parties and must notify the Federal agencies if controlled equipment will be disposed. The PWG will also continue to evaluate whether additional record-keeping or reporting by the LEAs would enhance the oversight and operations of the programs at issue, taking into account the costs and burdens of such additional obligations.

  With guidance from The United States Digital Service, the White House Office of Science and Technology Policy, and the Domestic Policy Council, the PWG will create a database that tracks information about controlled equipment purchased or acquired through Federal programs. This database will include information about, among other things, which LEAs have Federally-acquired controlled equipment in their inventory; the type of controlled equipment that was acquired by the LEA; from which federal agency the equipment was acquired; and whether the LEA is in violation of any statutory or programmatic requirement or otherwise subject to relevant sanctions. This database will be accessible by all PWG agencies and will be maintained collectively by the PWG. Consistent with the need to protect sensitive law enforcement information, and to the extent practicable, the information in the database should also be made publicly available.

The second function of the PWG is to harmonize Federal processes by developing consistent standards in oversight and other processes.

- *Ensure Government-wide criteria to evaluate requests for controlled equipment.* Consistency is essential at the front end of the acquisition process, especially with the implementation of Recommendation 3.1, which requires all Federal agencies to use the same criteria to evaluate requests for controlled equipment. The PWG will develop baseline standards and training so that Federal program managers can assess applications and requests in a consistent manner. After these standards are established, Federal agencies, with assistance from the Department of Justice, will be responsible for training their staff, State Coordinators or State Administering Agencies, and other relevant stakeholders who play vital roles in the acquisition process. In addition, DOJ will lead the PWG's regular efforts in examining Federal agency processes that review application criteria and will periodically make available to other PWG members for review and discussion a sample of such applications and adjudications to ensure consistency across Federal programs.

- *Ensure uniform standards for compliance reviews.* Consistency becomes even more important in Federal oversight functions as agencies continue to harmonize their processes. The PWG will develop uniform basic standards for what to investigate, how often compliance reviews should occur, how to evaluate detailed justifications and other parts of an LEA's application, how to screen for sufficiency of protocols and training, and other related issues. Additionally, the Federal Coordination and Compliance Section of the Department of Justice's Civil Rights Division, in its role of coordinating Federal enforcement and application of Title VI of the Civil Rights Act of 1964, will provide enhanced training to Federal Offices of Civil Rights on conducting rigorous civil rights compliance reviews of recipient-LEAs.

  The PWG will also facilitate a mechanism for those agencies lacking expertise to audit LEA procedures and practices involving controlled equipment from the perspective of civil rights, constitutional policing, and community impact. For example, the Office of Justice Programs is committed to entering into Memoranda of Understanding with other Federal agencies to increase their capacity to conduct this important auditing function.

Finally, the PWG will ensure that policies are in place to support Recommendation 5.2, which describes sanctions for programmatic and statutory violations. To continue to achieve increased consistency in Federal oversight processes, a violation of the controlled equipment program terms will result in suspension from all Federal controlled equipment acquisition programs for a minimum of 60 days and lasting until the violation has been resolved. The PWG will further specify the appropriate sanctions for more serious violations and their implications on the LEA's future participation in Federal equipment acquisition programs. And, as part of its information sharing function, the PWG will ensure that its member agencies are aware of LEAs that commit relevant programmatic or statutory violations sanctions.

* * * * *

Effective implementation of these recommendations depends significantly on robust Federal partnerships with law enforcement; civil rights and civil liberties groups; State, local, and Tribal government; State Administering Agencies and Coordinators; elected leaders; and members of the community. Therefore, within 45 days after the President receives these recommendations, the PWG will meet with stakeholders to further discuss the specifics of the recommendations and receive feedback potential approaches to implementing them. Additionally throughout the rest of Fiscal Year 2015, the PWG will continue to meet with these stakeholders in order to better identify training needs, adjust Federal processes, and develop relevant guidelines and resources. The PWG also will continue to evaluate how Federal equipment acquisitions programs can further prudent community policing practices and align with the recommendations put forward by the President's Task Force on 21st Century Policing. By the end of Fiscal Year 2015, the PWG will provide an update to the President on the progress of implementing the recommendations and any additional recommendations, suggestions, or clarifications to be considered based on stakeholder feedback.

The PWG's commitment to engage stakeholders extends beyond this fiscal year, as ongoing communication and input from the field are essential to ensuring that equipment provided to LEAs through Federal resources are appropriately used to protect and serve their communities and continue to preserve officer safety.

SUMMARY OF RECOMMENDATIONS

1. EQUIPMENT LISTS

RECOMMENDATION 1.1 — PROHIBITED EQUIPMENT LIST: The Prohibited equipment list identifies categories of equipment that should not be authorized for LEAs to acquire via transfer from Federal agencies or purchase using Federally-provided funds.

- **Tracked Armored Vehicles:** Vehicles that provide ballistic protection to their occupants and utilize a tracked system instead of wheels for forward motion.

- **Weaponized Aircraft, Vessels, and Vehicles of Any Kind:** These items will be prohibited from purchase or transfer with weapons installed.

- **Firearms of .50-Caliber or Higher**

- **Ammunition of .50-Caliber or Higher**

- **Grenade Launchers:** Firearm or firearm accessory designed to launch small explosive projectiles.

- **Bayonets:** Large knives designed to be attached to the muzzle of a rifle/shotgun/long gun for the purposes of hand-to-hand combat.

- **Camouflage Uniforms:** Does not include woodland or desert patterns or solid color uniforms.

RECOMMENDATION 1.2 — CONTROLLED EQUIPMENT LIST: The Controlled Equipment List identifies categories of equipment that LEAs may acquire by taking additional steps as described in Recommendation 3.1 and 3.2.

- **Manned Aircraft, Fixed Wing:** Powered aircraft with a crew aboard, such as airplanes, that use a fixed wing for lift.

- **Manned Aircraft, Rotary Wing:** Powered aircraft with a crew aboard, such as helicopters, that use a rotary wing for lift.

- **Unmanned Aerial Vehicles:** A remotely piloted, powered aircraft without a crew aboard.

- **Armored Vehicles, Wheeled:** Any wheeled vehicle either purpose-built or modified to provide ballistic protection to its occupants, such as a Mine-Resistant Ambush Protected (MRAP) vehicle or an Armored Personnel Carrier. These vehicles are sometimes used by law enforcement personnel involved in dangerous operating conditions, including active shooter or similar high-threat situations. These vehicles often have weapon-firing ports.

- **Tactical Vehicles, Wheeled:** A vehicle purpose-built to operate on- and off-road in support of military operations, such as a HMMWV ("Humvee"), 2.5-ton truck, 5-ton truck, or a vehicle with a breaching or entry apparatus attached. These vehicles are sometimes used by law enforcement in rough terrain or inclement weather for search and rescue operations, as well as other law enforcement functions.

- **Command and Control Vehicles:** Any wheeled vehicle either purpose-built or modified to facilitate the operational control and direction of public safety units responding to an incident. Command and Control vehicles provide a variety of capabilities to the incident Commander, including, but not limited to, the provision for enhanced communications and other situational awareness capabilities.

- **Specialized Firearms and Ammunition Under .50-Caliber (excludes firearms and ammunition for service-issued weapons):** Weapons and corresponding ammunition for specialized operations or assignment. This excludes service-issued handguns, rifles, or shotguns that are issued or approved by the agency to be used during the course of regularly assigned duties.

- **Explosives and Pyrotechnics:** Includes "flash bangs" as well as explosive breaching tools often used by special operations units.

- **Breaching Apparatus (e.g. battering ram or similar entry device):** Tools designed to provide law enforcement rapid entry into a building or through a secured doorway. These tools may be mechanical in nature (a battering ram), ballistic (slugs), or explosive.

- **Riot Batons (excluding service-issued telescopic or fixed-length straight batons):** Non-expandable baton of greater length (generally in excess of 24 inches) than service-issued types and are intended to protect its wielder during melees by providing distance from assailants.

- **Riot Helmets:** Helmets designed to protect the wearer's face and head from injury during melees from projectiles including rocks, bricks, liquids, etc. Riot helmets include a visor which protects the face.

- **Riot Shields:** Shields intended to protect wielders from their head to their knees in melees. Most are designed for the protection of the user from projectiles including rocks, bricks, and liquids. Some afford limited ballistic protection as well. Riot shields may also be used as an offensive weapon to push opponents.

RECOMMENDATION 2.1 — POLICIES AND PROTOCOLS: LEAs that acquire controlled equipment through Federal programs must adopt robust and specific written policies and protocols governing General Policing Standards and Specific Controlled Equipment Standards.

- **General Policing Standards** includes policies on (a) Community Policing; (b) Constitutional Policing; and (c) Community Input and Impact Considerations.

- **Specific Controlled Equipment Standards** includes policies specifically related to (a) Appropriate Use of Controlled Equipment; (b) Supervision of Use; (c) Effectiveness Evaluation; (d) Auditing and Accountability; and (e) Transparency and Notice Considerations.

- **Record-Keeping Requirement.** Upon request, LEAs must provide a copy of the General Policing Standards and Specific Controlled Equipment Standards, and any related policies and protocols, to the Federal agency that supplied the equipment/funds.

RECOMMENDATION 2.2 — TRAINING: LEAs that acquire controlled equipment through Federal programs must ensure that its personnel are appropriately trained and that training meets the following requirements:

- **Required Annual Training on Protocols.** On an annual basis, all LEA personnel who may use or authorize use of controlled equipment must be trained on the LEA's General Policing Standards and Specific Controlled Equipment Standards.

- **Required Operational and Technical Training.** LEA personnel who use controlled equipment must be properly trained on, and have achieved technical proficiency in, the operation or utilization of the controlled equipment at issue.

- **Scenario-Based Training.** To the extent possible, LEA trainings related to controlled equipment should include scenario-based training that combines constitutional and community policing principles with equipment-specific training. LEA personnel authorizing or directing the use of controlled equipment should have enhanced scenario-based training to examine, deliberate, and review the circumstances in which controlled equipment should or should not be used.

- **Record-Keeping Requirement.** LEAs must retain comprehensive training records, either in the personnel file of the officer who was trained or by the LEA's training division or equivalent entity, for a period of at least three (3) years, and must provide a copy of these records, upon request, to the Federal agency that supplied the equipment/funds.

RECOMMENDATION 2.3 — AFTER-ACTION REVIEW: (1) LEAs must collect and retain "Required Information" (described below) when law enforcement activity that involves a "Significant Incident" requires, or results in, the use of any Federally-acquired controlled equipment in the LEA's inventory (or any other controlled equipment in the same category as the Federally-acquired controlled equipment). (2) When unlawful or inappropriate police actions are alleged and trigger a Federal compliance review, and the Federal agency determines that controlled or prohibited equipment was used in the law enforcement activity under review, the LEA must produce or generate a report(s) containing Required Information.

- **"Significant Incident" Defined:** Any law enforcement operation or action that involves (a) a violent encounter among civilians or between civilians and the police; (b) a use-of-force that causes death or serious bodily injury[28]; (c) a demonstration or other public exercise of First Amendment rights; or (d) an event that draws, or could be reasonably expected to draw, a large number of attendees or participants, such as those where advanced planning is needed.

- **"Required Information" to Be Collected and Retained:** (a) Identification of controlled equipment used (e.g., categories and number of units of controlled equipment used, make/model/serial number); (b) description of the law enforcement operation involving the controlled equipment; (c) identification of LEA personnel who used the equipment and, if possible, civilians involved in the incident; and (d) result of controlled equipment use (e.g., arrests, use-of-force, victim extraction, injuries).

- **Format of Information Collection and Retention.** No new form or format is required as long as the Required Information is retained in a manner that is easily accessible and organized. For example, information about the use of controlled equipment can be included in an Operations Plan, detailed in officer daily logs, or described in use-of-force reports.

- **Record-Keeping Requirement:** LEAs must retain "Significant Incident" reports and Required Information for a period of at least three (3) years and must provide a copy of these records, upon request, to the Federal agency that supplied the equipment/funds. This information also should be made available to the community the LEA serves in accordance with applicable policies and protocols including considerations regarding the disclosure of sensitive information.

---

[28] See 18 U.S.C. § 1365(h)(3): "[T]he term 'serious bodily injury' means bodily injury which involves (A) a substantial risk of death; (B) extreme physical pain; (C) protracted and obvious disfigurement; or (D) protracted loss or impairment of the function of a bodily member, organ, or mental faculty."

RECOMMENDATION 3.1 — APPLICATION INFORMATION: In addition to application requirements mandated by individual Federal acquisitions programs, LEAs must submit information in the following categories for approval in all requests for controlled equipment:

- General description of the LEA.

- Detailed justification for acquiring the controlled equipment, including a clear and persuasive explanation of the need for the equipment and the appropriate law enforcement purpose that it will serve. An LEA's application for controlled equipment should describe any previous instance in which the controlled equipment was used in a manner that deviated from the detailed justification supporting the application for that equipment.

- Number of units of the requested controlled equipment that the LEA currently has in its inventory.

- Categories of other controlled equipment acquired through Federal programs during the past three (3) years that the LEA currently has in its inventory.

- Whether the requested controlled equipment currently could reasonably be accessed through loans or mutual assistance or mutual aid agreements.

- Certification that the LEA has adopted required protocols (see Recommendation 2.1) or will adopt those protocols <u>before</u> physical acquisition or purchase of controlled equipment or transfer of funds.

- Certification that the LEA has provided required training (see Recommendation 2.2) or will provide that training <u>before</u> physical acquisition or purchase of controlled equipment or transfer of funds.

- Evidence of civilian governing body's review and approval or concurrence of the LEA's acquisition of the requested controlled equipment.[29]

- Whether the requesting LEA has applied, or has a pending application(s), for this type of controlled equipment from another Federal agency during the current fiscal year.

- Whether any prior application for controlled equipment has been denied by a Federal agency during the past three (3) years, and, if so, the reason for the denial.

- Whether the LEA has been found to be in violation of a Federal civil rights statute or programmatic term during the past three (3) years and, if so, whether any disposition was reached or corrective actions were taken.

---

[29] For purposes of this criteria, a "governing body" is defined as the institution or organization that has direct budgetary oversight or fiscal/financial control over the requesting LEA.

RECOMMENDATION 3.2 — REGIONAL SHARING: The requesting LEA must indicate whether the requested controlled equipment is being acquired to provide a regional or multijurisdictional capability. In such cases, requesting LEAs must:

- Provide information regarding the size of the region, including the number and size of the LEA with access to the requested controlled equipment and the estimated population served.

- Certify that all LEAs in the regional sharing arrangement have adopted requisite protocols (see Recommendation 2.1) or will adopt those protocols <u>before</u> their personnel use the controlled equipment.

- Certify that all LEAs in the regional sharing arrangement have provided requisite training (see Recommendation 2.2) or will provide that training <u>before</u> their personnel use the controlled equipment.

- Certify that all LEAs in the regional sharing arrangement will adhere to the information collection and retention requirements (see Recommendation 2.3).

4. TRANSFER, SALE, RETURN, AND DISPOSAL OF CONTROLLED EQUIPMENT

RECOMMENDATION 4.1 — TRANSFER/SALE OF CONTROLLED EQUIPMENT TO OTHER LEAs: LEAs may transfer or sell any controlled equipment, except riot helmets and shields, to another LEA. Prior to finalizing any transfer or sales agreement, the transferor/seller-LEA must inform and obtain approval from the Federal agency that supplied the controlled equipment/funds. The acquiring-LEA must submit the same information (see Recommendations 3.1, 3.2) that was required of the transferor/seller-LEA to, and receive approval from, the Federal agency.

RECOMMENDATION 4.2 — TRANSFER/SALE OF CONTROLLED EQUIPMENT TO NON-LEAs: LEAs may transfer or sell only the following types of controlled equipment to non-LEAs: (a) Fixed Wing Aircraft; (b) Rotary Wing Aircraft; and (c) Command And Control Vehicles. All law enforcement-related and other sensitive or potentially dangerous components, and all law enforcement insignias and identifying markings, must be removed prior to transfer or sale. The transferor/seller-LEA must inform and receive approval from the Federal agency from which the controlled equipment or funding to purchase the equipment was acquired prior to the finalization of any transfer or sale.

RECOMMENDATION 4.3 — RETURN OF CONTROLLED EQUIPMENT: LEAs that acquire controlled equipment through DOD's 1033 program must abide by its requirements governing the return and/or disposal of controlled equipment.

RECOMMENDATION 4.4 — DISPOSAL OF CONTROLLED EQUIPMENT: LEAs must abide by all applicable Federal, State and local laws, regulations, and programmatic terms when disposing of controlled equipment. Prior to disposal, LEAs must notify the Federal agency that supplied the controlled equipment/funds.

5. OVERSIGHT, COMPLIANCE, AND IMPLEMENTATION

RECOMMENDATION 5.1 — PERMANENT LAW ENFORCEMENT EQUIPMENT WORKING GROUP: The members of the Working Group will form a permanent Federal Interagency Law Enforcement Equipment Working Group that meets regularly to support oversight and policy development functions for controlled equipment programs. The Permanent Working Group (PWG) will:

- Examine and evaluate the Controlled and Prohibited Equipment Lists for possible additions or deletions.

- Track LEA controlled equipment inventory.

- Ensure Government-wide criteria to evaluate requests for controlled equipment.

- Ensure uniform standards for compliance reviews.

- Track LEA sanctions and violations related to controlled equipment programs and usage.

RECOMMENDATION 5.2 — SANCTIONS FOR VIOLATIONS OF CONTROLLED EQUIPMENT PROGRAMS:

- **For Programmatic Violations.** For violations of any programmatic term or condition related to controlled equipment (e.g., failure to adopt required protocols, unauthorized transfers), the LEA will be suspended from acquiring additional controlled equipment through Federal programs for a minimum of 60 days. The suspension will continue until the Federal agency determines that the violation has been corrected. This does not prohibit a Federal agency from imposing other applicable sanctions according to applicable program parameters.

- **Statutory Violations.** For alleged violations of law, including civil rights laws, the matter will be referred for investigation to the Federal agency's Office of Civil Rights (OCR) or other appropriate compliance office, or the U.S. Department of Justice. If the investigation results in a finding that the LEA violated a civil rights or other relevant statute, the LEA will be sanctioned according to statute and/or the Federal agency's governing rules and policies. At a minimum, the LEA will be suspended from acquiring additional controlled equipment through Federal programs for a minimum of 60 days. The suspension will last until the Federal agency determines that the violation has been corrected.

APPENDIX A

EXECUTIVE ORDER 13688

Executive Order 13688—Federal Support for Local Law Enforcement Equipment Acquisition
January 16, 2015

By the authority vested in me as President by the Constitution and the laws of the United States of America, and in order to better coordinate Federal support for the acquisition of certain Federal equipment by State, local, and tribal law enforcement agencies, I hereby order as follows:

Section 1. Policy. For decades, the Federal Government has provided equipment to State, local, and tribal law enforcement agencies (LEAs) through excess equipment transfers (including GSA donations), asset forfeiture programs, and Federal grants. These programs have assisted LEAs as they carry out their critical missions to keep the American people safe. The equipment acquired by LEAs through these programs includes administrative equipment, such as office furniture and computers. But it also includes military and military-styled equipment, firearms, and tactical vehicles provided by the Federal Government, including property covered under 22 CFR Part 121 and 15 CFR Part 774 (collectively, "controlled equipment").

The Federal Government must ensure that careful attention is paid to standardizing procedures governing its provision of controlled equipment and funds for controlled equipment to LEAs. Moreover, more must be done to ensure that LEAs have proper training regarding the appropriate use of controlled equipment, including training on the protection of civil rights and civil liberties, and are aware of their obligations under Federal nondiscrimination laws when accepting such equipment. To this end, executive departments and agencies (agencies) must better coordinate their efforts to operate and oversee these programs.

Sec. 2. Law Enforcement Equipment Working Group. (a) There is established an interagency Law Enforcement Equipment Working Group (Working Group) to identify agency actions that can improve Federal support for the acquisition of controlled equipment by LEAs, including by providing LEAs with controlled equipment that is appropriate to the needs of their community; ensuring that LEAs are properly trained to employ the controlled equipment they acquire; ensuring that LEAs adopt organizational and operational practices and standards that prevent the misuse or abuse of controlled equipment; and ensuring LEA compliance with civil rights requirements resulting from receipt of Federal financial assistance. The Working Group shall be co-chaired by the Secretary of Defense, Attorney General, and Secretary of Homeland Security. In addition to the Co-Chairs, the Working Group shall consist of the following members:

      (i) the Secretary of the Treasury;

      (ii) the Secretary of the Interior;

      (iii) the Secretary of Education;

      (iv) the Administrator of General Services;

      (v) the Director of the Domestic Policy Council;

      (vi) the Director of the Office of National Drug Control Policy;

1

(vii) the Director of the Office of Management and Budget;

(viii) the Assistant to the President for Intergovernmental Affairs and Public Engagement;

(ix) the Assistant to the President for Homeland Security and Counterterrorism;

(x) the Assistant to the President and Chief of Staff of the Office of the Vice President; and

(xi) the heads of such other agencies and offices as the Co-Chairs may, from time to time, designate.

(b) A member of the Working Group may designate a senior-level official who is from the member's agency or office and is a full-time officer or employee of the Federal Government to perform the day-to-day Working Group functions of the member. At the direction of the Co-Chairs, the Working Group may establish subgroups consisting exclusively of Working Group members or their designees under this subsection, as appropriate.

(c) There shall be an Executive Director of the Working Group, to be appointed by the Attorney General. The Executive Director shall determine the Working Group's agenda, convene regular meetings, and supervise its work under the direction of the Co-Chairs. The Department of Justice shall provide funding and administrative support for the Working Group to the extent permitted by law and within existing appropriations. Each agency shall bear its own expenses for participating in the Working Group.

Sec. 3. Mission and Function of the Working Group. (a) The Working Group shall provide specific recommendations to the President regarding actions that can be taken to improve the provision of Federal support for the acquisition of controlled equipment by LEAs, which may include, to the extent permitted by law:

(i) developing a consistent, Government-wide list of controlled equipment allowable for acquisition by LEAs, as well as a list of those items that can only be transferred with special authorization and use limitations;

(ii) establishing a process to review and approve proposed additions or deletions to the list of controlled equipment developed pursuant to paragraph (i) of this subsection;

(iii) harmonizing Federal programs so that they have consistent and transparent policies with respect to the acquisition of controlled equipment by LEAs;

(iv) requiring after-action analysis reports for significant incidents involving federally provided or federally funded controlled equipment;

(v) developing policies to ensure that LEAs abide by any limitations or affirmative obligations imposed on the acquisition of controlled equipment or receipt of funds to purchase controlled equipment from the Federal Government and the obligations resulting from receipt of Federal financial assistance;

(vi) planning the creation of a database that includes information about controlled equipment purchased or acquired through Federal programs;

(vii) ensuring a process for returning specified controlled equipment that was acquired from the Federal Government when no longer needed by an LEA;

2

(viii) requiring local civilian government (non-police) review of and authorization for LEAs' request for or acquisition of controlled equipment;

(ix) requiring that LEAs participating in Federal controlled equipment programs receive necessary training regarding appropriate use of controlled equipment and the implementation of obligations resulting from receipt of Federal financial assistance, including training on the protection of civil rights and civil liberties;

(x) providing uniform standards for suspending LEAs from Federal controlled equipment programs for specified violations of law, including civil rights laws, and ensuring those standards are implemented consistently across agencies; and

(xi) creating a process to monitor the sale or transfer of controlled equipment from the Federal Government or controlled equipment purchased with funds from the Federal Government by LEAs to third parties.

(b) The Working Group shall engage with external stakeholders, including appropriate State officials, law enforcement organizations, civil rights and civil liberties organizations, and academics, in developing the recommendations required by subsection (a) of this section.

(c) The Working Group shall provide the President with an implementation plan for each of its recommendations, which shall include concrete milestones with specific timetables and outcomes to be achieved.

Sec. 4. Report. Within 60 days of the date of this order, the Working Group shall provide the President with any recommendations and implementation plans it may have regarding the actions set forth in section 3(a)(i) and (ii) of this order. Within 120 days of the date of this order, the Working Group shall provide the President with any additional recommendations and implementation plans as set forth in section 3 of this order.

Sec. 5. General Provisions. (a) Nothing in this order shall be construed to impair or otherwise affect:

(i) the authority granted by law or Executive Order to an agency, or the head thereof; or

(ii) the functions of the Director of the Office of Management and Budget relating to budgetary, administrative, or legislative proposals.

(b) This order shall be implemented consistent with applicable law and subject to the availability of appropriations.

(c) This order is not intended to, and does not, create any right or benefit, substantive or procedural, enforceable at law or in equity by any party against the United States, its departments, agencies, or entities, its officers, employees, or agents, or any other person.

BARACK OBAMA

The White House,
January 16, 2015.

[Filed with the Office of the Federal Register, 11:15 a.m., January 21, 2015]

NOTE: This Executive order was published in the *Federal Register* on January 22.

Categories: Executive Orders : Local law enforcement equipment acquisition, Federal support.

3

Subjects: Civil rights : Minorities :: Relations with police; Law enforcement and crime : Law Enforcement Equipment Working Group; Law enforcement and crime : local law enforcement equipment acquisition.

DCPD Number: DCPD201500033.

4

APPENDIX B

FEDERAL EQUIPMENT ACQUISITION PROGRAMS

The Federal Review identified multiple Federal agencies and programs that provide equipment to LEAs, either through direct transfers or through funding. Below is a list of the primary Federal sources of equipment or funding identified in the Federal Review, including a brief description of each program as it operated at the time of the review.

U.S. Department of Defense's (DOD) 1033 Program: The 1033 program allows the transfer, without charge, of excess DOD property (supplies and equipment) to LEAs. Excess property transferred to LEAs is designated in two ways — controlled or non-controlled. Controlled property includes small arms, night vision devices, High Mobility Multipurpose Wheeled Vehicles (HMMWVs or Humvees), Mine-Resistant Ambush Protected Vehicles (MRAPs), aircraft, and watercraft.

U.S. Department of Homeland Security's Homeland Security Grant Program (HSGP): The HSGP program provides funding to LEAs to assist agencies in building capabilities to prevent, protect against, mitigate, respond to, and recover from terrorist attacks, disasters, and other incidents in support of the National Preparedness Goal.[30] HSGP funds can be used to purchase equipment (including tactical vehicles, helicopters, and personal protective gear); however, the purchase of weapons and weapons accessories is prohibited within the programs.

U.S. Department of Justice's (DOJ) Justice Assistance Grant (JAG) Program: The JAG program provides States, tribes, and local governments with funding to support a range of program areas, including law enforcement operations. JAG funding may be used for the purchase of equipment within specific categories, such as technology, weapons, explosive devices, and delivery systems. JAG funds may not be used directly or indirectly to pay for vehicles (excluding police cruisers), vessels, aircraft, unmanned aerial vehicles/unmanned aircraft, aircraft systems, or aerial vehicles unless a waiver is requested.

U.S. Department of Justice (DOJ) Equitable Sharing Program (ESP): DOJ's ESP oversees the transfer and use of forfeited funds (via the Asset Forfeiture Fund) by LEAs. LEAs are permitted to spend ESP funding for law enforcement purposes, including the purchase of equipment and vehicles, subject to the appropriations and procurement rules and regulations of the State and local jurisdictions.

---

[30] The National Preparedness Goal defines what it means for a community to be prepared for all types of disasters and emergencies, including terrorist attacks.

U.S. Department of the Treasury Forfeiture Fund's Equitable Sharing Program (TFF): The TFF Program allows LEAs to request a share of forfeited assets by submitting a request to the TFF member agency completing the forfeiture. Funds may be used for any law enforcement purpose, including the purchase or lease of body armor, firearms, and vehicles.

General Services Administration's (GSA) Federal Surplus Personal Property Donation Program: GSA's Office of Personal Property Management assists Federal agencies in the disposition of property that is no longer needed by the respective Federal agency, including transfer to LEAs. Property items that may be transferred include firearms and specialized apparatus, including scientific devices and heavy machinery.

U.S. Department of Interior (DOI): For agencies within DOI, such as the U.S. Park Police, excess equipment, including weapons, can be transferred to LEAs. To transfer equipment to LEAs, the Department uses an acquisition management process.

APPENDIX C

LIST OF STAKEHOLDERS ENGAGED BY THE WORKING GROUP

American Civil Liberties Union

American Friends Service Committee

Asian Americans Advancing Justice

Brennan Center

Center for Policing Equity

Charles County Sheriff's Office

Dignity in Schools Campaign

Drug Policy Alliance

Fraternal Order of Police

Friends Committee on National Legislation

Hispanic American Police Command Officers Association

Human Rights Watch

Interagency Board

International Association of Campus Law Enforcement Administrators

International Association of Chiefs of Police

International Association of Emergency Managers

Los Angeles County Sherriff's Department

Lawyers' Committee for Civil Rights

Leadership Conference on Civil Rights

Major Cities Chiefs Association

Major County Sheriffs' Association

NAACP Legal Defense and Education Fund

National Animal Care and Control Association

National Asian Peace Offices' Association

National Association for the Advancement of Colored People

National Association of Attorneys General

National Association of Civilian Oversight of Law Enforcement

National Association of Police Organizations

National Association of School Resource Officers

National Association of Social Workers

National Association of State Agencies for Surplus Property

National Congress of American Indians

National Criminal Justice Association

National Emergency Management Association

National Latino Law Enforcement Organization

National Native American Law Enforcement Association

National Organization of Black Law Enforcement Executives

National Sheriff's Association

New Jersey State Police

Omega Research Foundation

Police Foundation

Tampa Police Department

U.S. Conference of Mayors

United Methodist Church - GBCS

University of Wisconsin Police

Urban Institute

Ventura County Sheriff's Office

Virginia Department of Criminal Justice Services

Washington State Patrol